ULTIMATE STICKER COLLECTION

I am Master Eon, your guide. Skylands is indeed a magical place, but beware, for Darkness also lurks here. An evil Portal Master named Kaos has destroyed the Core of a Light, an ancient, magnificent device that has protected our world for many years. Now he wants to rule Skylands! Together, we must find the legendary heroes who can defeat Kaos, the Skylanders. Each Skylander has unique abilities and powers linked to one of the eight elements—Air, Earth, Fire, Water, Magic, Technology, Life, and Undead. Come and learn more about these amazing heroes, the world of Skylands, and the enemies who threaten our universe.

Greetings, young Portal Master, and welcome to Skylands.

HOW TO USE THIS BOOK

Read the captions, then find the sticker that best fits in the space. (Hint: check the sticker labels for clues!)

Don't forget that your stickers can be stuck down and peeled off again.

There are lots of fantastic extra stickers to create your own scenes throughout the book.

DK

LONDON, NEW YORK, MELBOURNE, MUNICH, AND DELHI

Written by Catherine Saunders
Edited by David Fentiman
Designed by Liam Drane and Owen Bennett

First published in the United States in 2013 by DK Publishing
345 Hudson Street, New York, New York 10014

10 9 8 7 6 5 4 3 2
002–192413–Jun/13

Page design copyright © 2013 Dorling Kindersley Limited

ISBN: 978-1-4654-0986-7

Color Reproduction by Altaimage in the UK
Printed and bound in China by L-Rex

Discover more at www.dk.com

MAGIC SKYLANDERS

Magic is the the most mysterious of all the ancient Elements, as no one knows where it came from. Its essence is a special oil, known as Quicksilver, which flows through every living thing in Skylands. Some of the mightiest heroes in Skylands are able to harness the power of Magic.

Spyro
This fearless, fire-breathing hero is a legend in Skylands. His flaming breath is too hot for most enemies!

Dark Spyro
When Spyro harnesses dark Magic he becomes Dark Spyro. However, dark Magic is dangerous and he must be careful!

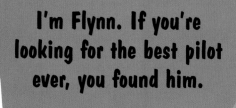

I'm Flynn. If you're looking for the best pilot ever, you found him.

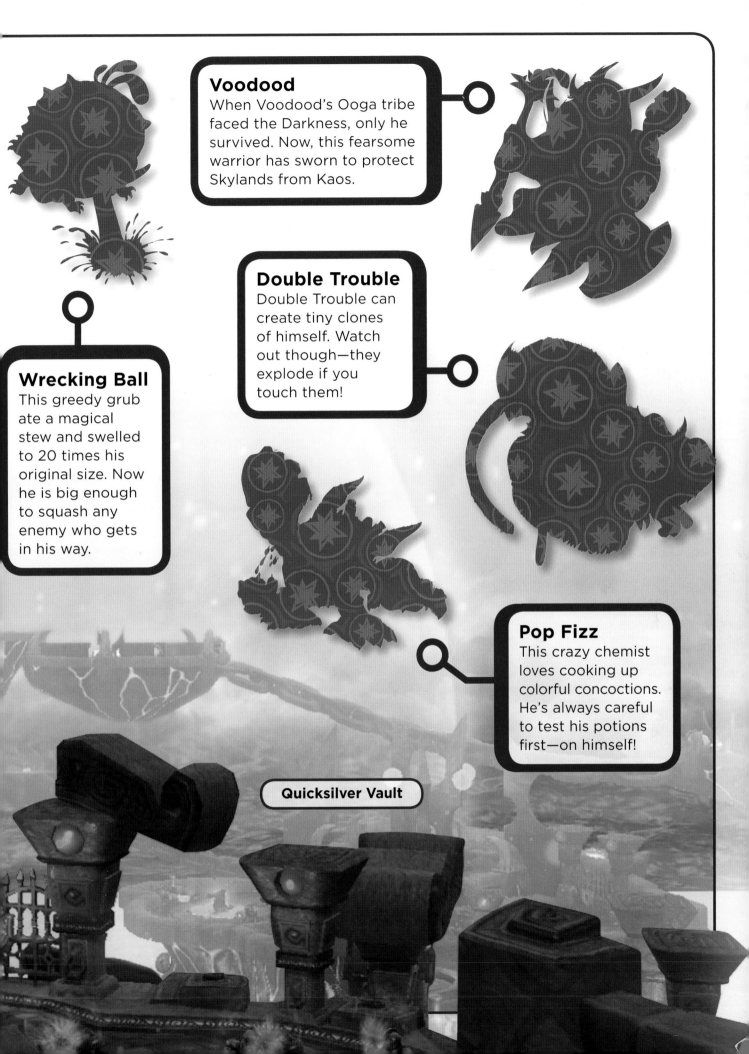

Voodood
When Voodood's Ooga tribe faced the Darkness, only he survived. Now, this fearsome warrior has sworn to protect Skylands from Kaos.

Double Trouble
Double Trouble can create tiny clones of himself. Watch out though—they explode if you touch them!

Wrecking Ball
This greedy grub ate a magical stew and swelled to 20 times his original size. Now he is big enough to squash any enemy who gets in his way.

Pop Fizz
This crazy chemist loves cooking up colorful concoctions. He's always careful to test his potions first—on himself!

Quicksilver Vault

EARTH SKYLANDERS

Some of the toughest Skylanders possess the ability to harness the Element known as Earth. These fearsome warriors are famous for their strength, stamina, and courage. They have the power to use rocks, crystals, and even the Earth itself against anyone who threatens Skylands.

Bash
He can't fly, but this brown rock dragon can definitely roll! When Bash curls up into a spiky, armored ball, it's time for his enemies to take cover.

Miner Hat
Wearing this Miner Hat will protect a hero from danger if they are going underground.

Stonetown

Dino-Rang

Here comes double dino trouble! Daring Dino-Rang has mastered the art of fighting with twin boomerangs.

Terrafin

This brawny boxer looks terra-fying, but he is a hero. In fact Terrafin would just love to get Kaos in the ring—and knock him right out!

Bone Head

It might look odd, but wearing the Bone Head gives a Skylander greatly increased speed.

Flashwing

This purple and blue gem dragon uses the power of crystals. She can fire crystal laser blasts from her tail.

Prism Break

Only two things matter to Prism Break—saving Skylands and protecting his cave full of gems. Few of Kaos's minions would dare take on this grumpy rock golem.

AIR SKYLANDERS

Heroes linked to the Air Element are able to harness the fearsome forces of nature. These skilled warriors gather their powers from extreme weather, such as wind and lightning. When these warriors are in action, the forecast for their enemies is stormy, with a strong chance of defeat.

Jet-Vac
Unlike most other Sky Barons, Jet-Vac doesn't have wings. This flying hero takes to the skies with the aid of a powerful vacuum device instead.

Top Hat
This elegant Top Hat can be found in the region of Skylands known as Stonetown.

I'm Cali. So you're ready to try a Heroic Challenge, huh? Well, let me warn you right off the bat, they're TOUGH. Like me.

Whirlwind
Part dragon and part unicorn, Whirlwind is a unique creature in Skylands. She has the ability to fly and can also shoot rainbows from her horn.

Lightning Rod
Strike! Storm Giant Lightning Rod likes to throw huge lightning bolts at his foes. He is very brave, and he wants people to know about it!

Warnado
This tornado-loving turtle can spin so fast that it makes his enemies dizzy. Warnado can also summon tornadoes to use against his foes.

Stormy Stronghold

Sonic Boom
Sonic Boom is a mythical creature known as a griffin. When she screeches it is so loud that no one can bear to be near her.

Propeller Cap
If heroes find themselves at Sky Schooner Docks, they should locate this cool Propeller Cap.

FIRE SKYLANDERS

Stand well back—Skylands' hottest heroes are a major fire hazard! These flaming warriors harness the Element of Fire to burn, singe, scorch, and smoke out their enemies. Their sizzling strength can rarely be matched—except, perhaps, by those who use the power of Water.

Sunburn
Part dragon and part bird, Sunburn is one of the hottest heroes in Skylands. He loves to scorch his enemies with his flaming breath.

Fez
Wearing this Fez, a hero can face Drow spearmen with confidence and style.

Eruptor
Don't make this hot-headed lava monster angry! Eruptor spews out fireballs of molten rock and boiling hot lava whenever he gets mad.

Combat Hat
When in battle, wearing this protective Combat Hat is a very sensible idea indeed.

Ignitor
When this knight was tricked into putting on some enchanted armor, he became a fire spirit. Now known as Ignitor, he wields a flaming sword.

Rocket Hat
If a hero needs a little extra speed, this Rocket Hat is the perfect fit.

Hot Dog
Hot Dog is a hero's best friend. The brave fire pup can turn himself into a comet and launch himself at any foes. Good boy!

Flameslinger
Flameslinger possesses a magical bow, which can fire flaming arrows. This fiery elf can hit virtually any target, even when wearing a blindfold.

Lava Lakes Railway

WATER SKYLANDERS

The Element of Water can be used in a variety of ways. Some Water warriors are sea creatures. These aquatic heroes are great swimmers and they fight with water-powered weapons. Others harness Water differently. These cool heroes use Water in the form of ice and face their foes with frozen weapons.

Pan Hat
It's not very fashionable, but wearing this Pan Hat can double a hero's armor strength, and Elemental power.

Slam Bam
This artistic yeti likes to trap his foes inside ice sculptures. If that fails, Slam Bam uses his four powerful fists.

Gill Grunt
Thanks to his harpoon gun and jet pack, Gill Grunt is a pretty slick hero. However, his most dangerous weapon is his terrible singing!

Leviathan Lagoon

Birthday Hat
Wearing the Birthday Hat gives a Skylander a great gift—extra speed and increased Critical Hit power.

Wham-Shell

Wham-Shell is the toughest crustacean in Skylands. His mace weapon is known as the Troll Cracker, after one of his most famous victories.

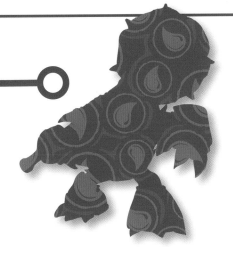

Chill

Chill is searching for the lost Snow Queen. Meanwhile, she protects Skylands with a range of ice weapons.

Napoleon Hat

This Napoleon Hat is useful for any aspiring generals fighting Kaos in Leviathan Lagoon.

Zap

He was born into a family of water dragons, but raised by electric eels. That's why Zap possesses dragon speed with added electricity!

UNDEAD SKYLANDERS

Come and meet the warriors associated with the dark Element—Undead. Many of these brave heroes have been exposed to evil or taken a trip to the world of the Undead. They must use their element wisely—it can give them great powers, but it can also lead them toward darkness.

Cynder
Cynder, a violet dragon, breathes dark electricity instead of fire. She was saved from a life of evil by another legendary dragon, Spyro.

Fancy Hat
This Fancy Hat might not suit every Skylander, but you can find it in Stormy Stronghold.

Spy Gear
The Troll Warehouse is a dangerous place, but a clever hero can use this Spy Gear to find their way out.

Chop Chop
This undead skeleton warrior used to work for the ancient Arkeyan race, but nowadays Chop Chop uses his sword and shield to defend Skylands.

Ghost Roaster

Ghost Roaster was a regular chef until he fell into the Valley of the Undead. Now he is a ghoulish gourmet who loves eating ghosts!

Fright Rider

When two heroes combine, they can form a fearsome fighting force. Rider is an Undead elf and Fright is his skeletal ostrich steed.

Hex

Hex became one of the Undead when she visited the Underworld. She possesses powerful dark Magic, but is a trusted Skylander.

I'm Master Eon's assistant, Hugo. What I feared is coming to pass! The Darkness is taking over the land! We MUST hurry . . . .

Plunger Head

If a Skylander is brave enough to wear a Plunger on his or her head, it will give them a handy power boost.

TECH SKYLANDERS

The cleverest heroes in Skylands are drawn to the Element known as Technology. These wise warriors like to build things, invent stuff, and experiment with new weapons. They use their brains as well as their brawn in the battle to protect Skylands and keep it safe from the Darkness.

Sprocket
As an engineer, Sprocket knows how stuff works. She has constructed her own battle armor and an array of powerful weapons.

Trigger Happy
Trigger Happy's two favorite things are gold and guns. In battle, this gun-toting gremlin doesn't use bullets, he uses gold coins.

Drill Sergeant
This ancient Arkeyan machine uses his drills to shoot or ram anyone who attacks Skylands. Drill Sergeant is a simple hero who just likes to follow orders.

Drobot
Drobot is not a typical dragon. He prefers finding out how things work to flying, and has built his own robotic suit.

Use the spare stickers to create your own amazing battle scene!

LIFE SKYLANDERS

Some Skylanders are closely connected with nature, so they draw upon the Element of Life. Many of these elemental warriors are plant-based creatures, who use their own greenery as a weapon, while others can create or control the kinds of plants that will make their foes tremble in fear.

Stealth Elf
Stealth Elf attacks quickly and quietly, just like a ninja. She can also create copies of herself to fool unsuspecting enemies.

Shroomboom
Shroomboom is a fun guy and a sharp shooter with a slingshot. However, he has a fear of ending up as Kaos's pizza topping!

I'm Arbo. Isn't nature wondrous? I could just stand out here all day, absorbing moisture and sunlight. But I guess that's because I am a tree.

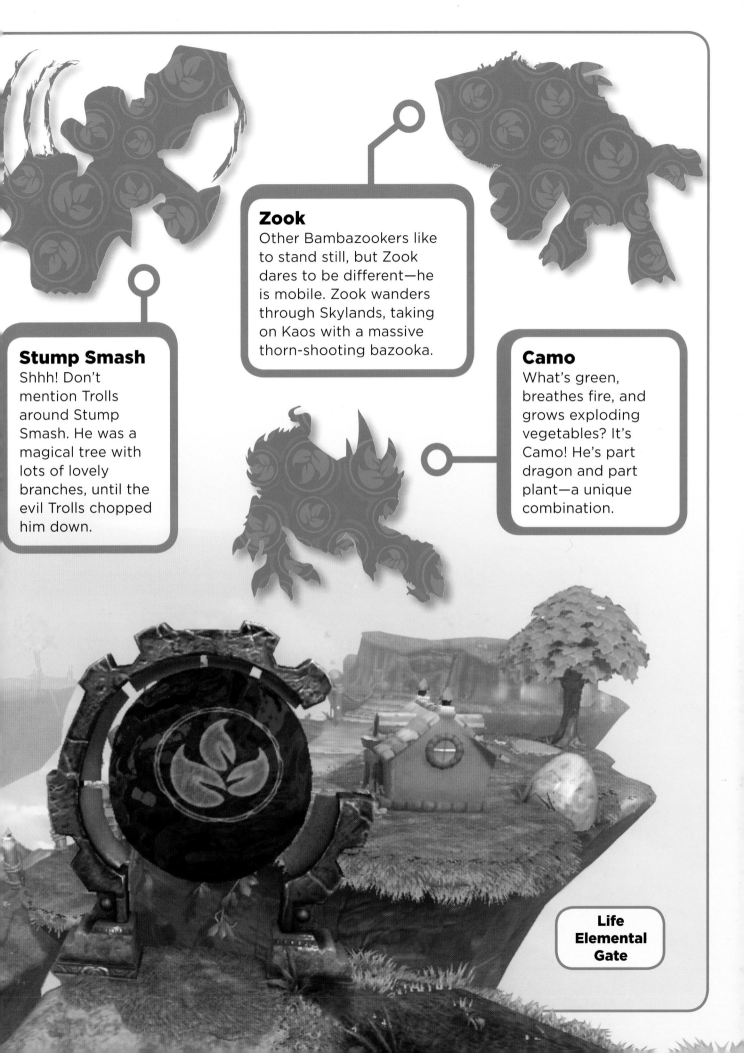

Zook

Other Bambazookers like to stand still, but Zook dares to be different—he is mobile. Zook wanders through Skylands, taking on Kaos with a massive thorn-shooting bazooka.

Stump Smash

Shhh! Don't mention Trolls around Stump Smash. He was a magical tree with lots of lovely branches, until the evil Trolls chopped him down.

Camo

What's green, breathes fire, and grows exploding vegetables? It's Camo! He's part dragon and part plant—a unique combination.

Life Elemental Gate

MEET THE GIANTS

No one had seen the ancient heroes known as Giants for centuries. In fact, many people doubted that they even existed—but thankfully those people were wrong. The Giants were buried deep underground on Earth, but they are back now, and ready to join the battle against Kaos.

Bouncer
Being an All-Star Roboto Ball player made Bouncer a celebrity, but he likes to be a hero both on and off the playing field.

Thumpback
Hero ahoy! Thumpback used to be a pirate, but he preferred fishing to finding treasure. This whale-like creature defends Skylands with his giant anchor.

Tree Rex
Thousands of years ago Tree Rex was just a huge, old tree growing in a forest. But his soil was poisoned, so he mutated into a lumbering Giant.

Eye Brawl
What happens when you cross a headless Giant with a flying eyeball? You get one of the most powerful heroes ever known—Eye Brawl.

Hot Head
Stand well back! Hot Head is ready to burst into flames at any moment. This Fire Giant is one hot hero . . . .

GIANTS IN BATTLE

There are many awesome heroes in Skylands, but few can match the strength and raw power of the Giants. They are twice as big as any other hero and are able to perform special feats of strength that only they can pull off. There aren't many enemies who can take on a Giant!

Swarm
Swarm lived in a hive with 9,000 members of his family, until he grew too big. He is a giant wasp, with giant stings!

Ninjini
When she is not protecting Skylands with her double swords and orbs of magic, Ninjini likes relaxing inside an enchanted bottle.

Crusher
Crusher is happiest when he is smashing rocks into tiny pieces. He wields a powerful hammer, which is also great for crushing enemies.

Use the spare stickers to fight against the evil Arkeyan King!

HANDY HELPERS

Not everyone in Skylands can be a hero. However, everyone has a part to play in defending their magical world from the threat of the Darkness. Come and meet some of the creatures who, in their own special ways, help Master Eon and the brave Skylanders keep Skylands safe.

General Robot
This military robot is in charge of the Mabu Defense Force, which helps to protect Skylands from Kaos.

Cali
Cali is Skylands' most fearless explorer. She often helps to prepare Skylanders for dangerous missions.

Flynn
Mabu pilot Flynn isn't the cleverest creature in Skylands, but he can always count on the support of his biggest fan—himself.

Perilous Pastures

Gurglefin

If a hero needs to get to Oilspill Island, Gurglefin will take them in his ship, just as long as the mission isn't too dangerous!

T-Bone

T-Bone is happy to take heroes to the Underworld. He is dead already, so not much scares him—except spiders, that is.

Persephone

A fun-loving fairy, Persephone loves dancing, and also likes helping heroes to develop their abilities.

Diggs

This helpful Molekin is a skilled engineer and train driver, but he has very bad eyesight.

Arbo

This small, tree-like creature loves sunlight. He can also be a useful guide on missions to forest worlds.

Hugo

Master Eon's assistant, Hugo, knows all about the history of Skylands. He prefers books to battles.

WEIRD WILDLIFE

There are many weird and wonderful creatures in Skylands, but there are plenty of downright nasty ones, too. Some are dangerous, some are scary, but most are just really annoying. Get to know some of the creepy, crawly, crazy creatures that sensible Skylanders would rather avoid.

Chompy
These little green monsters pop up everywhere! They bark like dogs, and like to bite, too.

Chompy Pod
The best way to destroy a Chompy is to wreck its Pod before it can hatch.

Gargantula
These huge, black spiders are terrifying. When a Gargantula catches someone, it reels them in using its webs.

Stump Demon
These gigantic evil trees will eat any Skylanders they can catch, and devour Chompies to heal themselves!

Cruncher
Crunchers are pesky blue critters related to Chompies. They like to latch onto heroes with their sharp teeth.

Leviathan
This large fish has a huge appetite. In fact, Leviathan has been known to devour whole villages!

Nauteloid
Nauteloids are small crustaceans who like to attack Skylanders by charging at them, nose first.

Spider Swarmer
Spider Swarmers specialize in running at heroes and then exploding, which is why they're often called Skitterbooms!

Fat Belly
Fat Belly spiders are not overeaters, they just have bellies full of acidic spider goo, which they like to spew over unsuspecting targets.

Moon Widow
Moon Widow spiders aren't dangerous. However, they can sometimes accidentally trap Skylanders in their sticky webs.

Armored Chompy
An Armored Chompy is tougher than a regular Chompy, but just as annoying.

Corn Hornet
These nasty insects like to sting heroes. They look like wasps, except for their dragon wings.

THE TROLLS

Even an evil mastermind can't take over Skylands all by himself—he needs loyal minions to help him. Kaos chooses the Trolls to aid him in his quest. They're not very smart, but they like making weapons and they absolutely love blowing stuff up, chopping down trees, and drilling for oil.

Grenadier
These pesky Grenadiers are armed with grenades and they love to lob them at brave heroes.

Blaster
Blaster Trolls specialize in rapid-fire energy blasts. However, their guns quickly run out of energy and always need charging.

Gun Snout
This Troll-shaped tank can shoot bullets from its nose, so it is known as a Gun Snout.

Mark 31 Tank
The Mark 31 tank is the Trolls' toughest armored vehicle. It is very hard to destroy!

Greasemonkey
Greasemonkeys don't have weapons, so they like to stay safe inside tanks, such as Gun Snouts.

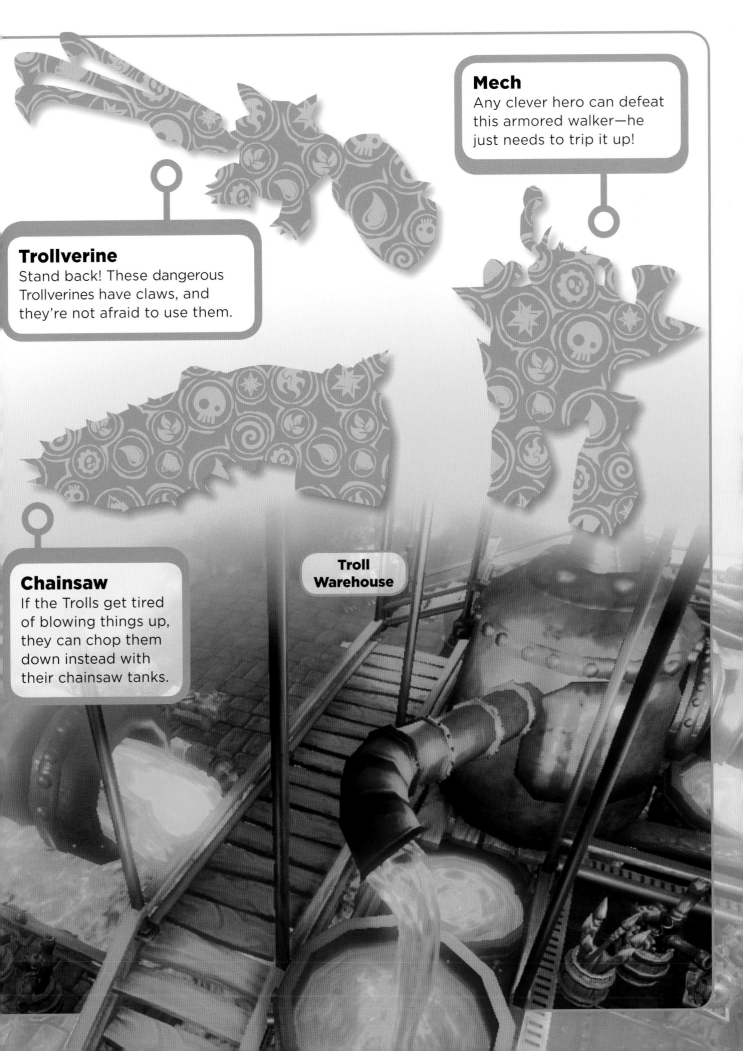

Mech
Any clever hero can defeat this armored walker—he just needs to trip it up!

Trollverine
Stand back! These dangerous Trollverines have claws, and they're not afraid to use them.

Chainsaw
If the Trolls get tired of blowing things up, they can chop them down instead with their chainsaw tanks.

Troll Warehouse

THE DROW

Like other elves, the Drow love nature, and these greeny-blue creatures are prepared to fight to preserve the natural order of things. Unfortunately, they have also turned to the Darkness and are loyal to the evil Portal Master, Kaos. Skylanders had better watch out for these mean little guys.

Spearman
Drow Spearman wield sharp red blades, mounted on long shafts. Their weapons are bigger than they are!

Goliath
These guys are pretty big, for elves. They like to form groups and charge at their foes.

Archer
What's that rustling in the trees? It is probably a Drow Archer ready to take aim.

Armored Goliath
Goliath Drows fight with two shields, one on each arm. As the Goliaths charge, spikes appear on the shields.

Armored Lance Master
It takes a pretty strong elf to wield a spear this big while wearing heavy armor.

Witch
The Drow Witches specialize in throwing sharp disc weapons over long distances. They seem to have an unlimited supply of them.

Blitzer Bully
These special Goliath Drows carry wizards known as Spell Punks on their backs. The wizard is ready to heal the Goliath if it gets injured.

Lance Master
Lance Masters are even tougher than regular Drow Spearmen. They wear red armor and swing their lances around in a twirling attack.

Drow Zeppelin

THE ARKEYANS

Thousands of years ago, the Arkeyans ruled Skylands with an iron fist—literally! They were an advanced civilization able to fuse magic and technology together to create a powerful robot army. They were also very evil, but luckily the Giants rose up to defeat them!

Crackler
These small, armored robots like to shock their enemies, and create illusions of themselves to confuse any attackers.

Jouster
Jousters specialize in short-range combat. They like to fight one-on-one against heroes, swinging their lethal double-ended spears.

Gyrocopter
Gyrocopters are even deadlier than Defense Drones. They have three propellers, greater firepower, and they can also carry passengers.

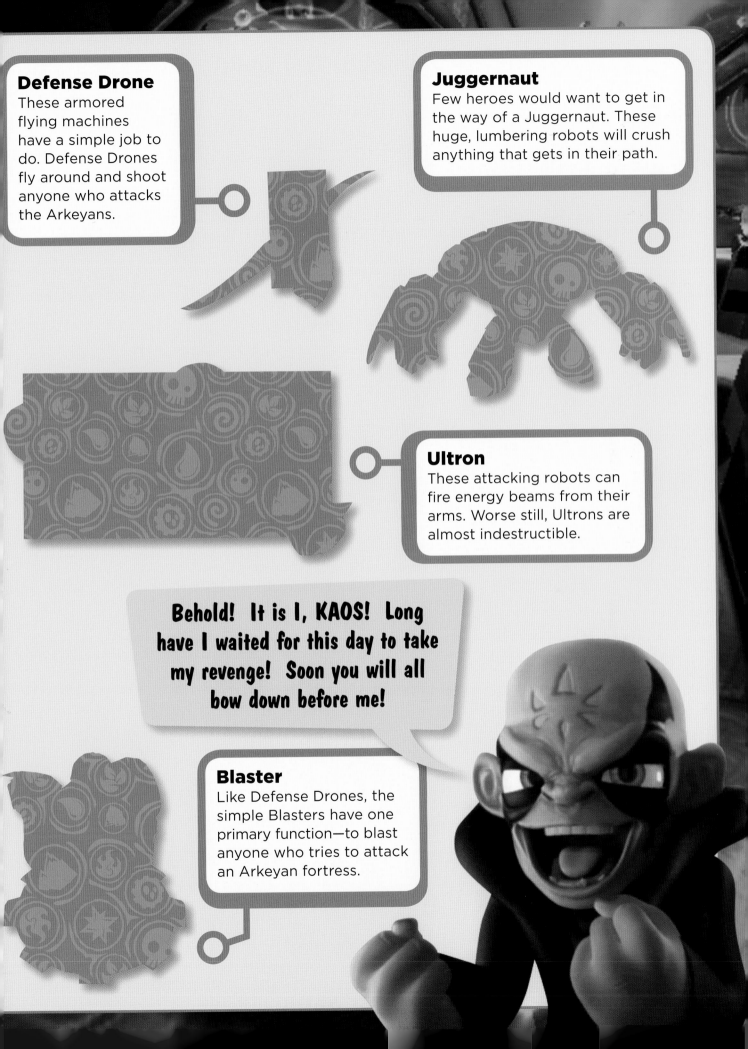

Defense Drone
These armored flying machines have a simple job to do. Defense Drones fly around and shoot anyone who attacks the Arkeyans.

Juggernaut
Few heroes would want to get in the way of a Juggernaut. These huge, lumbering robots will crush anything that gets in their path.

Ultron
These attacking robots can fire energy beams from their arms. Worse still, Ultrons are almost indestructible.

Behold! It is I, KAOS! Long have I waited for this day to take my revenge! Soon you will all bow down before me!

Blaster
Like Defense Drones, the simple Blasters have one primary function—to blast anyone who tries to attack an Arkeyan fortress.

VILE VILLAINS

When it comes to being evil in Skylands, Kaos is the Number 1 bad guy. He's clever, powerful, and determined to rule Skylands by any means necessary. However, Kaos is not the only villain in the universe. Some evil-doers work for him, but others just enjoy being nasty.

Kaos

This evil Portal Master destroyed the Core of Light, and spread the Darkness throughout Skylands. He uses powerful magic and commands many evil minions, such as the Trolls and Drow.

Captain Dreadbeard

Captain Dreadbeard is the meanest pirate on the Pirate Seas. When he's not buccaneering, the scurvy seadog loves playing Skystones. However, he usually cheats.

Kaos' Kastle

Stone Golem

The Stone Golem is a rock monster with the ability to make rocks rain down from the sky. He likes to use them to crush heroes!

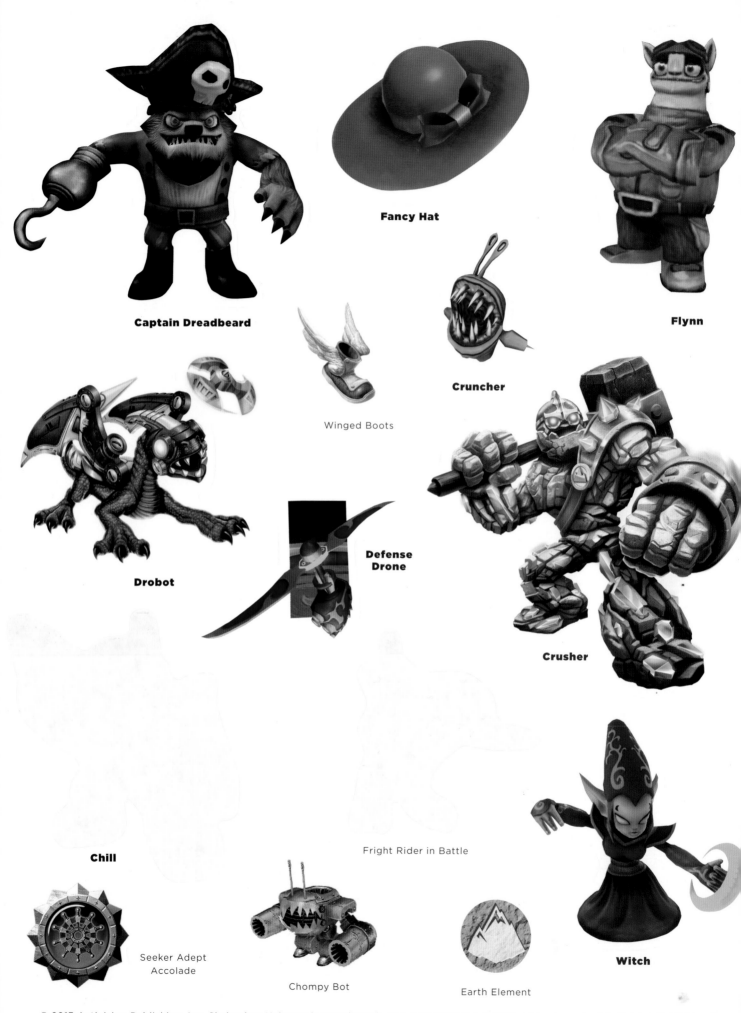

Captain Dreadbeard

Fancy Hat

Flynn

Cruncher

Winged Boots

Drobot

Defense Drone

Crusher

Chill

Fright Rider in Battle

Seeker Adept
Accolade

Chompy Bot

Earth Element

Witch

Plunger Head

Pan Hat

Juggernaut

Magic Element

Captain Accolade

Dragonfire Cannon

Tech Spell Punk

Savior of Skylands Accolade

Armored Goliath

Chainsaw

Boulder Bowler

Cyclops Chopper

Air Element

Nauteloid

Hot Head

Zap

Cali

Mark 31 Tank

Spy Gear

Birthday Hat

Water Element

Pop Fizz

Gurglefin

Flashwing

Anvil Rain

Chop Chop

Jouster

Sergeant Major Accolade

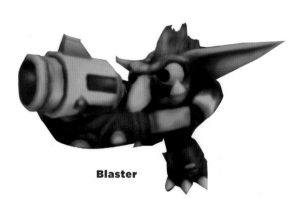

Blaster

Tree Rex

Gigantic Hero Accolade

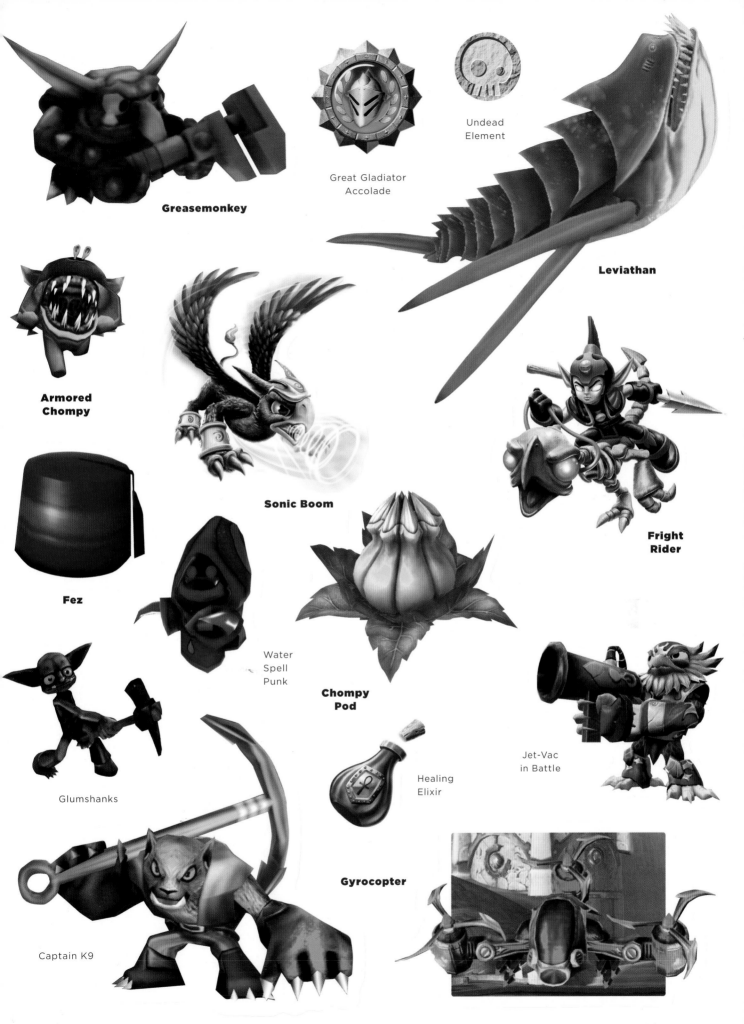

Greasemonkey

Great Gladiator
Accolade

Undead
Element

Leviathan

**Armored
Chompy**

Sonic Boom

**Fright
Rider**

Fez

Water
Spell
Punk

**Chompy
Pod**

Jet-Vac
in Battle

Glumshanks

Healing
Elixir

Gyrocopter

Captain K9

T-Bone

Undead Spell
Punk

Empire of Ice

Ninjini

Gill Grunt

Hex

Hugo

Treasure Hunter
Accolade

Nightmare Avenger
Accolade

Life Element

Propellor Cap

Mech

**Blitzer
Bully**

Kaos

Ghost Roaster

Trog Wanderer

Spyro

Golden Gear

Miner Hat

Bone Head

Jet-Vac

Hint Scholar
Accolade

Stone Golem

**Armored Lance
Master**

Fire Element

Fat Belly

Chompy

Diggs

Master Eon

Ambassador
Accolade

Ghost Pirate
Swords

Vial of
Quicksilver

Rotten Robby

Blobbers

Tech Element

Bouncer

Skull Mask

Fashionista Accolade

Camo

Trog Pincher

Napoleon Hat

Crackler

Arbo

Lance Master

Warnado

General's Hat

Dark Spyro

Chief Scholar
Accolade

Rocket Hat

Moon Widow

Sprocket

Archer

Shroomboom

Earth Spell
Punk

Chill in Battle

Wham-Shell

Blaster

Goliath

To the Max Accolade

Trollverine

Wardrobe Saint
Accolade

Eye Brawl

Gun Snout

Sunburn

Hidden Treasure

Lightning Rod

Flame Imp

Weapon Master

Master of Skyland
Accolade

Eruptor

Bag O' Boom

Spearman

Corn Hornet

Combat Hat

Elite Agent
Accolade

Dino-Rang

Tiki Hat

Bash

Shrine Statue

Double Trouble

Trigger Happy

Ultimate
Completionist
Accolade

Dragon's Peak

Gargantula

Pop Fizz in Battle

Life Spell Punk

Persephone

Ignitor

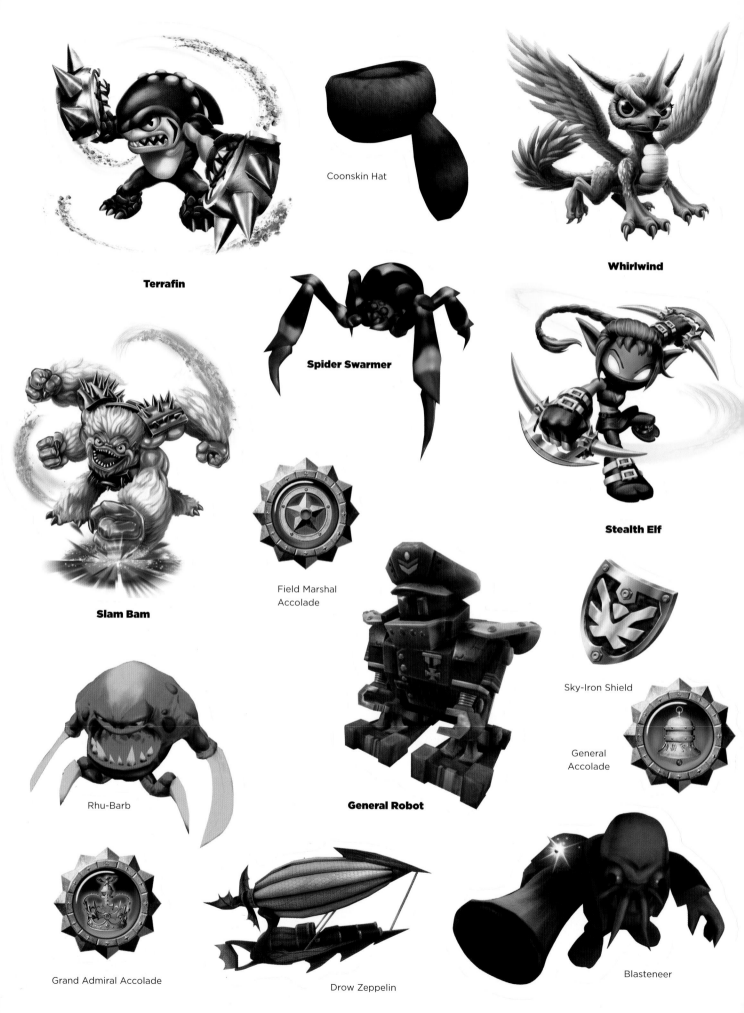

Coonskin Hat

Whirlwind

Terrafin

Spider Swarmer

Stealth Elf

Slam Bam

Field Marshal
Accolade

Sky-Iron Shield

General
Accolade

Rhu-Barb

General Robot

Grand Admiral Accolade

Drow Zeppelin

Blasteneer

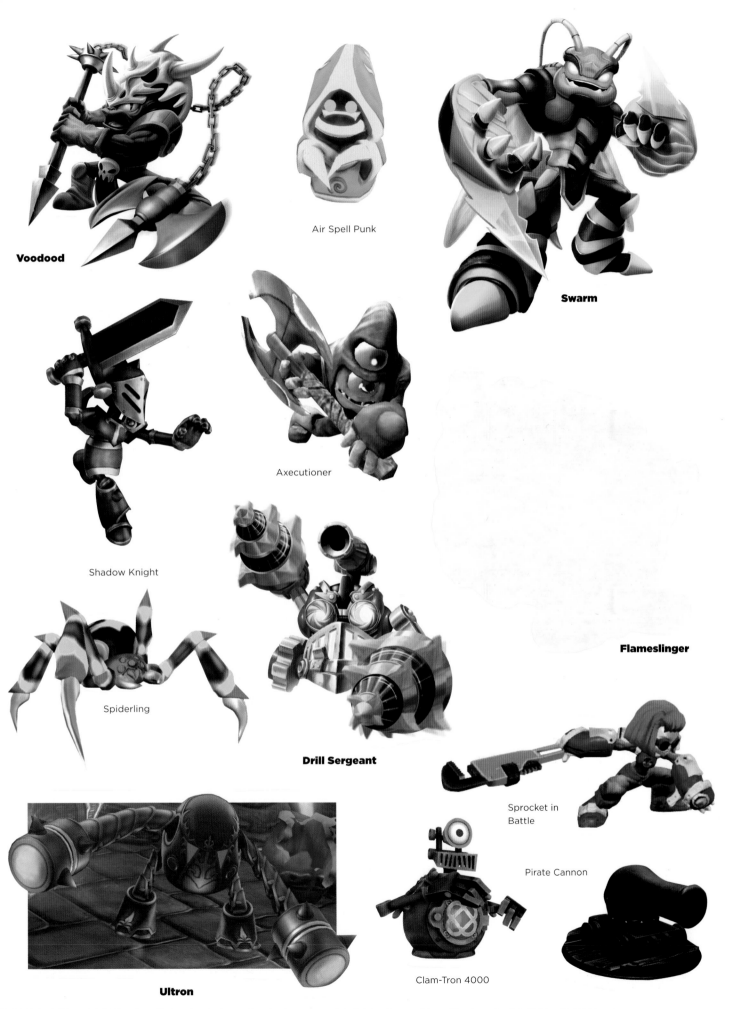

Voodood

Air Spell Punk

Swarm

Shadow Knight

Axecutioner

Flameslinger

Spiderling

Drill Sergeant

Sprocket in
Battle

Pirate Cannon

Ultron

Clam-Tron 4000

Colonel
Accolade

Time Twist
Hour Glass

Prism Break

Squidface Brute

Hot Dog

Stump Smash

Faithful Trio
Accolade

Cynder

Fire Spell Punk

Timidclops

Shadow Duke

Lava King

Grenadier

Thumpback

Commander
Accolade

Squiddler

Auric

Magic Spell
Punk

Crucible for
the Ages

Trogmander

Zook

Top Hat

Wrecking Ball

Clam

Pirate Ship

Snuckles

Flashwing
in Battle

Stump Demon

© 2013 Activision Publishing, Inc. Skylanders Universe is a trademark, and Activision is a registered trademark of Activision Publishing Inc.

EXTRA STICKERS

EXTRA STICKERS

EXTRA STICKERS

EXTRA STICKERS

EXTRA STICKERS

EXTRA STICKERS

EXTRA STICKERS

EXTRA STICKERS

EXTRA STICKERS

EXTRA STICKERS

EXTRA STICKERS

EXTRA STICKERS

EXTRA STICKERS

EXTRA STICKERS

EXTRA STICKERS

EXTRA STICKERS